voice carried my family

ALSO BY ROBERT SULLIVAN

POETRY
Captain Cook in the Underworld
Star Waka
Piki ake!
Jazz Waiata

CO-EDITED
Whetu Moana: Contemporary Polynesian Poems in English,
with Albert Wendt and Reina Whaitiri.

FOR CHILDREN AND YOUNG ADULTS
Māui: legends of the outcast, illustrated by Chris Slane
Weaving earth and sky: myths and legends of Aotearoa, illustrated by Gavin Bishop

ROBERT SULLIVAN

voice carried my family

AUCKLAND
UNIVERSITY PRESS

I dedicate this book to Anne, Temuera and Eileen

Some of these poems appeared in the following NZ publications: *Landfall,*
Parihaka: the art of passive resistance (Wellington: Morrison Trust, 2000),
Best New Zealand Poems 2002 (online); and in the USA: *Ploughshares, Mānoa, Tinfish*

First published 2005

Auckland University Press
University of Auckland
Private Bag 92019
Auckland
New Zealand
www.auckland.ac.nz/aup

© Robert Sullivan, 2005

ISBN 1 86940 337 1

Publication is assisted by ⓢcreative
nz

Cover design: Christine Hansen
Cover photograph: Paul Snow-Hansen

Printed by Publishing Press, Auckland

Contents

I FOR GODS AND WAKA

Chant Waka   2
Bird Waka   3
Wakas   4
London Waka   6
Tāne retrieves the baskets of knowlege   8
Gods and Oysters   10
Voice carried my family, their names and stories   11
A Biography   12
Te ao hurihuri   14
South Point, Hawai'i   15

II FOR SHADOWS

13 ways of looking at a blackbirder   18
Omanaia   21
Resolving the shadows of home   23

III FOR THE OCEAN OF KIWA

1 The Great Hall   26
2 Tupaia   27
3 Mai   28
4 Queen Charlotte Sound   29
5 New Information   30
6 Bubbling ground   31
7 The Wide Shot   32
8 A Resolution   33
9 I / Eyes / Ae   34
10 The Northeast Passage Home   35

11 Ocean Birth   36
12 Rapanui Easter Island   38
13 I see red, I see red, I see red   39
14 Pearl Harbor   40
15 Captain Cook   41
16 mind the gap   42
17 it's all been done before, eh   43

IV   FOR FIRES
Song   46
Boyle Abbey   47
Heart Wounds   48
Take   49
Kowhaiwhai   50
Love Poem   52
close to you   53
mother and child   54
stepping stones   55
the view from my office   56
purgatory   57
Ahi Kā – The House of Ngā Puhi   58
the crackling page   60
Poems from Another Century, for Parihaka   61
our country   65

Notes   66

I

For Gods and Waka

Chant Waka

Dive coral people
shell necklaced lovers' nacre
to pick up black pearls
hold them in a word's breath
with lips underwater oh

Bird Waka

On Mānoa stream
white headed blue black feathers
glide – head reflected
underwater like a pond
feet cross to faster water

Wakas

i

Russian dolls shuffled
like a distracted lover
mumbling crap to keep
him happy – impossible
leaps over the possible

ii

curve of mounting her
eyes sideways in the blue thought
– not today my friend
and I'm impossibly wrapped
in the complete injustice!

iii

yet look to the stream
it burbles and swerves, snivels
and laughs as it flirts
with desire that burns water
into air – lost energy

iv

heat does that as flames
in their licking wound the skin –
veins bubble and scald –
even vaporising blood
won't share all the feelings here

v

in my heart leaves fell
neatly into an autumn
stack for burning all
and all and all and all these
till I stopped sobbing, lit them

London Waka

On 6 February 1870, the waka *Pono* sailed down the Thames
in the belly of the steamer *Troy*. The crew slipped their canoe out

of the tin hull under the cover of a yellow fog. They killed
on the first night – lobbed a bomb into a corner pub.

Other waka joined them as vessels from the South Seas
arrived with their booty. Soon a canoe fleet started marauding

Southend, and the rebels commandeered some vessels.
On they steamed to London. They fired the heavy artillery every day

for months. The blighters even had a cheek to fire at the West End!
The great bells of Big Ben fell down. Westminster caved.

In a trice the capital fell to the Maori who sacked the seat
without mercy. A marquess and a baronet were returned to the Bay of Islands

and paraded at the Waitangi Marae. Spoils of war.
But I'm glad to report the Maori returned the Elgin Marbles,

and the Assyrian friezes, retrieved the woven waka sail
first taken by Cook and housed in the Museum of Mankind.

The Maori forged alliances with a quarter of the people of the planet
by emptying the spoils of the British Museum, the Victoria and Albert,

the Ashmolean. Palestine free! Rhodesia free! South Africa free! Kenya free!
India free! Canada free! Ireland free! Australia free! West Indies free! Aotearoa free!

Governor Heke has announced that the colony – England – is sending
shipments of frozen lamb to New Zealand, and potatoes to Ireland, instead of troops.

We expect they will benefit from limited self-government in the long term.
A restoration project is underway to ensure the survival of their language.

Tāne retrieves the baskets of knowlege

I shimmied my way up the thick vine like a cord
plugged into heaven – electricity crackled down the line
between my hands, reflexes tightening the fingers – I took it
as a message from the gods, onwards! So up I went

clapping hands ankles knees to the breeze
as the cord arced left and right in the sky –
I climbed this thought all the way until I reached
Io the Parentless One, the supreme deity.

Without moving his lips he asked me how I got there.
'Oh great lord, it was a thought
that carried me here, and a thought that will
return me to my family.' Young man,

my creatures helped you here: the wind god
Tāwhirimatea launched your body and your thought;
I let you visualise the vine; now you are here
so that you may carry these baskets of thoughts

back to your family so they may call themselves gods,
and launch houses of knowledge. Take all three
and share them. If I could I'd pour them in your ears
but there's too many: they could spill over the minds

of evil men so take great care of them: secrets
to split the atom; secrets to rule a country with expensive housing,
health care, and forcing people to fight; secret pollutants;
secrets to clone people; secret hate. Have care

for your return, young man. 'But lord, where is the vine
                                    I dreamt of?'
'E Tāne, you see that arch in the clouds? go through that door,
it leads to the eleven lower heavens to your home
on the ground.

'Your vine disappeared when you saw the baskets.
They contain all the thinking you will ever need.
Don't get me wrong – I liked your thought – maybe
your descendants will find one too and also climb it.'

Gods and Oysters

What made Tangaroa believe he was a local?
Was it the sea touching these shores and all the earth with rain
or its abstinence?
Was it the chanting as the waka crew prised from their teeth
sloppy oysters – the oohhhs and aahhhs? the slobber?
Was it the way he leapt out of the waka and said, 'Yes!
Build me a temple on this spot – this will be my centre –
the world's navel is here!' Was it Tangaroa's eyes registering
belief in the eyes of his subjects? Belief! Belief! Belief!
as he smacked his lips and parted another oyster with his teeth.

He was the king of the oysters and all the shores they slept on:
King of Oysters on the seabed; King of Oysters on the headlands;
King of all the oyster deities lining river mouth gums
bleeding into the sea. His tongue felt the pearl and his lips
revealed it – wet and black; he tucked it in his pocket
with the others. On and on they popped in there:
pile of pearls in his trousers, pile of shells on the rocks.

Only his tongue cared to remember the question. His face twisted,
eye whites rolled up, and out the tongue-tip leapt:
'Eeee yaaa ha ha!' the licker said. 'You're a local.'

Voice carried my family, their names and stories

Their names and fates were spoken.
The lands and seas of the voyage were spoken.
Calls of the stroke at times were spoken.
Celestial guidance, sightings, were spoken.
Prescriptions – medical and spiritual – were spoken.
Transactions – physical and emotional – were spoken.
Family (of), leaders (to), arguments, were well spoken.
Elders (of), were well spoken.
Burials were spoken.
Welcomes at times were spoken.
Futures lined up by pasts, were spoken.
Repeating the spoken were spoken.
Inheritance, inheritors, were spoken.
Tears at times were spoken.
Representations at first were spoken.
The narrator wrote the spoken.
The readers saw the spoken!
Spoken became unspoken.
[Written froze spoken.]

A Biography

We held them to catch
this. The glass shelves
are spotlighted to catch
green curves, green layering
and prices – but I only want the singing.

The song is ancient. Flecks in the stones
show their breeding, which
is important. But turn the lights out
and there is only singing. This
stone is one of the singers:

I watch the top waters
flow – catching the spare light
I lie here waiting
for you to hold me.

I am life and its shape,
shaped to you.
The song filling your heart,
moving the blood of this stone.

Creatures flow in the space
around the stone, some control
the way they tumble. When
there is light the stone is here.
When there is no light the stone

is here. The presence of the stone
fills us, ribs our hearts as we tumble.
We have been tumbling a long time.
When we land, we land on other stone –
lining prison floors, reinforcing

citadels that launder
clothes and cheques.
But even in the gravel
that makes the grey stone,
there is greenstone.

What else keeps singing the song?
We hear it – yet there is nothing to see.
Our pounamu sings.
Even in the gravel there must be
flecks of pounamu.

We cannot leave, we came from here.
We cannot go back – this is our England.
We bring pounamu up from our rivers.
The greenstones on our chests
are the life of this land.

Te ao hurihuri

The everchanging presence of the earth
is a term, te ao hurihuri, it shifts
like a dancer turns and turns.

The everchanging term is the presence
of the earth, te ao, like it shifts a dancer,
hurihuri, turns and turns.

Like turns the everchanging turn
of the term is te ao hurihuri,
the earth – a dancer shifts.

It shifts the earth, te ao hurihuri,
a term like a dancer.

It shifts te ao hurihuri, a term.

A term, hurihuri, in te ao.

Te ao hurihuri.

South Point, Hawai'i

On the Big Island, where the ocean voyaging waka left
for Tahiti, perhaps Aotearoa, we watched the mooring stones:

smoothed by water, smoothed by hands,
carved out to moor the waka.

We felt the spirits soar in the wild wind around us,
wind strong enough to break the wind mills

littering the field. How they soared. We felt them.
This spiritual harbour. We felt them more than the great heiau

lying in ruins, more than the native information centre
with its statue of a woman in chains.

How could the ancestors know such desecration
would arrive in this place? Such sadness.

And yet their spirits soar here. They fly here.
We flew here and flew, our minds and hearts flew.

II

For Shadows

13 ways of looking at a blackbirder

i

my shadow has come to take my place
again – has become daring – stands in the brightest sun
where people proclaim he is like me

ii

what right does a shadow have to be a person?
a shade flits from person to bird to tree
depending on the light's angle
the time of day the clouds up there

iii

but it's hard to argue with shadows
 – everyone has a shadow, look!
and everyone's on the greyscale
 – can't argue with that

iv

my shadow has my shape but not my colour
passes over ground like earth across the moon
doesn't whisper waits for me to make all the sounds
when I move my shadow moves

v

his boat has rum spiked with poppy
and a hold with iron grates only shadows
may pass through

vi

my shadow is an imposter
picked the stitches of the one I cared for since a boy
and cast it all the way to South America
this shadow annoys me
makes rude gestures when I want poetry
oh to sit with Plato's shadows instead of that one

vii

how can my shadow call that poetry?
doesn't my shadow know anything?

viii

I have decided I must have signed a contract in my sleep
with a blackbirding devil
that nailed this shadow to my hands and feet

ix

my shadow confesses a love for my culture
through a microphone
in the audience I roll out a smile

x

I tell myself to be generous with the shadow
looking for an identity
looking for a moko in the darkness
looking for the traffic light at the blood's intersection
looking for the slight in this

xi

truth is I could like this shadow
that talks like my brother even looks like him in the dark

xii

in the purging wasteland shantihs
let peace rain down and sink the blackbirders
claw off the nailed shadow from me

xiii

free at last from irony and its grating
I have my shadow back
the one stitched to me by my mother and father
the one handed down *tuku iho tuku iho*
shadow finding land
shadow only of the absence of light
and I am glad the other has returned to its owner
to show the nails dipped in and torn out of my blood
for shadows never bleed

Omanaia

Before we left for Hawai'i we went to visit my grandmother,
her grave at Omanaia in the Hokianga district.

We found a caretaker and he took us through, wondering why
her stone wasn't in the Ngakuru cemetery across the other side.

It took a while. He looked at the names and wondered if she'd be
in this family's section, or that family's section,

and every name made me think of a story my mother told me.
I won't tell you exactly where her grave is because of my shadow

who would like to know everything about me, and commit identity theft.
I sense this shade even from across the equatorial water.

Her grave is very close to Papahurihia's, of whom someone else I knew
wrote, and took his story, took the spiritual capital

the great prophet and our family built for generations.
He was an expert of Ngā Puhi and not just a divine.

I try to think good thoughts about these shadows who would tell my stories,
our family stories. So I will think the following good thoughts, addressed to them:

you wrote these things out because you love the Maori people and our culture.
You wrote these things out because you desired them in some way,

wanted other people to see them in their brilliance.
You wrote these things with love and honour in your hearts.

Perhaps I hold too tightly to my family, and our stories,
because I sense your desire and it frightens me?

I think of my grandmother lying in *her* grave
and want it to remain so. Hers. Face to face with our ancestor.

Resolving the shadows of home

night so deep the river stones wept

night and shadows made one

objects confused with spirits

and day a jug yet to be poured from the sky

The news off the Net:
  – abolish Maori representation
  – Te Heuheu sacked by the Opposition
  – foreshores confiscated forever

I swept the pen erratically across black paper –

words couldn't fill the night

III

For the Ocean of Kiwa

1 The Great Hall

Stained-glass figures: Cook and Marsden,
a WWI veteran, foundational figures of Canterbury,
and the launch, launching Cook's caulked vessel – *CC
in the Underworld* – I dedicated her to my grandfather
and read a poem. Finally, with glasses raised
we launched her.
                      Still I feel like I'm with the *Endeavour*
making repairs off the Great Barrier,
fothering the hull with the sails of the story:
we had spyscopes and Venus to celebrate,
James's soul to interrogate, the cosmos, enlightenment,
Banks behaving like a bonobo, but a problem,
a problem that scratches the sails as they form their skin
of tar.
             And so I bring a new lens, two, a pair of eyes
for the mission: Tupaia's, and another pair, Mai's,
two other pairs: Koa and Te Weherua's. Polynesian eyes
on Cook's several crews.
                  I looked at the stained glass
in Canterbury's Great Hall, and noticed
one unidentifiable Maori at the lowest right
on whose shoulders stood all the others.

2 *Tupaia*

Who am I to extol Tupaia? Star navigator. Great chief.
Cartographer of a chunk of the Pacific Cook claimed his own?
Loving Tupaia of the Arioi? Who am I to say these things?

My ancestor took the name of a Tahitian: the King Pomare.
My ancestor was a priest of the Ngā Puhi nation and a prophet: Papahurihia.
My ancestor was a leader and star navigator too: Kupe.
My ancestor was named for a bird: Ngāmanu.

One ancestor was a nun at Boyle Abbey, now in ruins in Ireland.
Another was acting governor of the colony. My ancestors
meet your ancestors. We press noses and share breath: ha!

And ha again. Ha the breath again. Ha and ha and ha. Breath.

These people are here and meet you.

Tēnei te mihi atu ki a koe, e te ariki. 'This greeting is to you, high lord.'

Your story. Your story and your eyes are yours.

Our people, wherever the *Endeavour*
first touched land cried out for you on Cook's return:

'Tupaia! Where is Tupaia?!' Starman of Rangiātea, ancestral heaven.

3 Mai

You're in the public domain – perhaps I could claim
your story through your eyes? You were a Polynesian man,
a hit with the ladies, a good mate of Banks
Lord Sandwich and Dr Burney. His Majesty at Kew received you –
what a stir, an entertainment to be cited in the *Gentleman's Magazine*:
so precious that unlike many 'savages'
HM saw to it you were inoculated against the smallpox.
Why not? Why can't I tell your tale, slip under your skin?

I can see you at the opera, watching Sandwich banging on the kettledrums,
admiring Handel's oratorio, his last work before his blindness (according
to the *Boston Globe*): *Jephtha*: I wonder if you understood
the need to sacrifice a daughter on a divine whim?
Being shocked by the Duke of Manchester's electrifying machine
was a mean trick, however. Not amusing.
I can see you in national velvet listening to the speech from the throne
at the House of Lords. Oh my! A big noter.

I also hear you were a dab shot at home,
became a hero, rescued your island from invaders.

But I can't. I just can't take the middle of your throat.
Who would I pay for the privilege?

I'm trying to make sense of this shadow
that follows me across my shoulder.
Why this discomfort? I've heard it said
that I should not listen to 'enemies of the imagination'.

Whose image? Who is imagining?

4 Queen Charlotte Sound

Two boys hopped on board there: Te Weherua,
and his younger companion, Koa. Mind the gap!

The boys wept when land dropped away
– seasick, and the first Maori ever

to leave Aotearoa that way.
I can only imagine the song they sang:

Ko te mokemoke
Nā te wehenga
Āpōpō rā, āpōpō rā,
Ka kite ai.

Oh the loneliness
Since separation
Tomorrow, tomorrow
We will see them.

Koa was ten years old amid topmasts and mainstays,
mizzen sails and jibs. The first to learn these things.

After his tears Te Weherua kept good company with the officers.
They helped to make the *Resolution* Polynesian.

5 New Information

Out to sea we ate bitter leaves called sauerkraut
to stave off rotten gums, teeth falling seventy leagues,

our bones cracking to pieces. Ha! This scurvy is fearsome
but I've seen many diseases now – hands who'd clutch

their cocks and cry in poxy raves. I've seen plague scars
like boathook gouges, limbs nibbled by sharks, rope burn and lash marks.

We, Koa and I, had better eat our greens. You see I miss my father
and will eat anything they tell me is good for me so I will see him.

The crew talk about Davy Jones a bit.
He has all his teeth.

6 Bubbling ground

Resolution's sails brush my hair – I like the feeling, wind soft as my mother,
canvas rough like my father's face. The ocean is our bubbling ground

and land the puddles. Valleys come and go in a trice,
mountains churn to troughs, fish are souls that leap out of water,

our vessel a lumbering elephant – unlike the sleek Tahitian waka
skimming the sea. An elephant on the ocean indeed! Trumpet

to talk through, cannons and muskets angled off her back,
sail-cloth on her tusks and the lash to keep the beast moving.

A jumbo fancy. Yet we (Te Weherua, Koa and I) remember stories
passed from Tupaia's lips to Banks's to Mai's – how a bird descended

from the heavens, became an island. And now all our islands
are unsettled, become menageries for visitors, the land

less solid than the sea. Now we clamber aboard with their goats,
chickens, pigs, sheep, turkeys, ducks and cattle. Some of these

they drop off. Once Cook burnt a village to the ground
because someone stole two goats. But he is a good man. He's a chief.

7 *The Wide Shot*

I'm so ill trinkets do nothing for me: what's a nail when there's no trees to bang it home,
no women to impress?! I heard Tupaia died in Batavia. Mai told me. He said his mate

Banks wept when telling him. He had a fever from bad air in the colony. The star
navigator ground into the open sewers of a hellhole. Yet Sir Joseph felt in the passing

of his friend a serenity, *noblesse*, of a cosmic magnitude: in bleak Australia where
his translation skills died, he dreamt stars with aborigines; so I dreamt Tupaia found

home stars glowing like pinpricks through the sun's black veil – light and shade cast across
the ocean. Now Koa and I are cast with Mai but we think he likes red cloth too much.

8 A Resolution

Young Koa looks at the spirals in the waves, then
into the tattooed spirals of Te Weherua's face.

Some of the *Resolution* are fishing; metal barbs glint
as lines are tossed – ha! how do they do it?

come all this way to fish? Koa composes another song,
follows the rules of waiata, eight vowel sounds to every half-line:

> *I can barely count these rude sounds*
> *but I will make music of them.*
> > *I am Te Weherua's friend,*
> *charged to keep him company*

> *far from our own Queen Charlotte Sound.*
> > *I feel like Kupe splitting up*
> *north and south islands with his adze,*
> > *such is the strait between two worlds*

> *Te Weherua and I've dived*
> > *into. We're in a fix and Mai*
> *is too concerned with his mirror:*
> > *'Banks said!' – it's insufferable.*

> *Still when I gaze at my comrade*
> > *spirals on his skin comfort me:*
> *messages from home – full of song*
> > *our brothers' and sisters' voices.*

9 I / Eyes / Ae

Aye aye Captain they sing, swearing
                below the songline. They've come
a very long way they tell us
                often. We sympathise, sigh, watch

their faces, time their damp sobs as
                they clutch blonde locks, then take hanks
to examine in the comfort
                of our homes upon our return.

Their sailing technology is
                inferior, but we can learn
so many things: fill our flax kits
                with good and evil. We observe

sailors' spirits rise and fall with
                rum. They fight a bit. Their breath stinks
while their clothes cry out for fire. Yet
                we like them – from our hiding place

they're entertaining away from
                the lash. Our mate Mai's a greaser,
name drops, harps on about the King:
                HM likes Mai's voice, hat, and face. . . !

I want my father's company
                afloat on waves so wide and deep
all the stacked ancestors – feet
                to broad shoulders – couldn't break them.

10 *The Northeast Passage Home*

Let's leave our crew for a minute and fast-forward
to the final trip home: the grim recovery of Cook's parts,

a chunk of thigh here, a burnt bit of palm there,
all the venerated giblets and victuals of a god. His several burials at sea.

Then the crew's flight to the Russian Far East and the Romanovs' Governor:
now that's a dynasty with a punch! Europe all the way

through Asia. The news crossed the steppes in a flash and arrived
in the admirals' hats, the imperial crown of St Edward,

his sweet wife Elizabeth's bonnet, dear England's chattering caps.
Christendom chastened him. That's what you get when you're a wannabe

god. When ya forget ya sposed to worship the lord. When ya forget
ya ain't descended from the heavens like . . . hmm . . . lest we forget.

11 Ocean Birth

With the leaping spirits we threw
          our voices past Three Kings to sea –
                    eyes wide open with ancestors.

We flew air and water, lifted
          by rainbows, whales, dolphins thrashing
                    sharks into birthways of the sea's

labour: Rapanui born graven
          faced above the waves – umbilical
                    stone; Tahiti born from waka:

temple centre of the world;
          Hawai'i cauled from liquid
                    fire: the goddess Pele churning

land from sea: born as mountains;
          Aotearoa on a grandmother's
                    bone – Maui's blood to birth leviathan;

Samoa, Tonga, born before
          the names of the sea of islands,
                    before Lapita clay turned to gourd,

before we slept with Pacific
          tongues. Chant these births Oceania
                    with your infinite waves, outrigged

waka, bird feasts, and sea feasts,
          Peruvian gold potatoes.
                    Sing your births Oceania.

Hold your children to the sky
           and sing them to the skyfather
                      in the languages of your people.

Sing your songs Oceania.
           Pacific Islanders sing! till
                      your throats are stones heaped as temples

on the shores for our ancestors'
           pleasure. PI's sing! to remind
                      wave sand tree cliff cave of the songs

we left for the Moana Nui
           a Kiwa. We left our voices
                      here in every singing bird –

trunks like drums – stones like babies –
           forests fed by our placentas.
                      Every wave carries us here –

every song to remind us –
           we are skin of the ocean.

12 Rapanui Easter Island

I watch the bloodied crosses lumber from the Americas –
slavers come to preach the joy of master–slave relations here

to the stone masters of the waves – graven faces cracked,
tilted, mute – hauled and chipped from Polynesian eyes

to live and die here near forever. Near is enough for me –
head held up by an island's shoulders – body treading water.

And the spirits of these? Where will they leap? Every head's
a cliff-face covered in dusty make-up waiting for an avalanche:

so many faces to choose from for the masters.
So many places to leap.

13 *I see red, I see red, I see red*

The sharpness of the eastern vertex
cuts me as I trail a red finger up to Hawai'i
and back to Aotearoa completing the triangle.

Red is the noblest cloth used by Cook/Kuki/Lono
to make best friends with all Polynesia –

he drowned our leaders in red
anointed young upstarts too as if it were
SPQR purple. We did anything and everything
for red. Sang any song fit for a god.

Our islands blushed red like Tiberian Capri –
gourds upended like goblets filled with menstrual filigree.

We still push our red barrows.

14 Pearl Harbor

I meant this to be a poem about Aotearoa
so forgive me.

The Americans have lined their guns in front of the palace,
suspended the constitution, arrested the Queen. Not Victoria.

Nor Elizabeth. Lili‘uokalani. Inheritor
of the kingdom that rose when Lono came.

Bearer of the world's creation story, *The Kumulipo*,
recited when Kuki/Cook came.

But now when I think of the Congress that betrayed her
faith I think of Pearl Harbor

on the silver screen, wonder at the power of America
to make losses seem like victories. What power

to reach back into the throat of history
and make her words gurgle sweetly.

15 Captain Cook

Didn't we get rid of him? There are far too many statues, operas
and histories. If only I could be a brown Orwell – a Maori Big Bro,
find every little caption card in every European museum and scrub it out:
change the wording to, 'This was given to Captain Cook as a token of friendship
and should be buried with him', OR 'This was temporarily given to Captain Cook
and would have been expected to be returned on his death', OR 'Well, actually, Captain
Cook stole this', OR 'The Captain exchanged this for something vastly inferior in value –
ha ha for him!' But even as an extra large bro I suspect the lies are superglued.
The empire that sent him to his death three times has its hero.

16 *mind the gap*

out of the underworld and into the dazzling daylight of Oxford St
couture and bustle out and about – red buses at sauntering pace –
Charing Cross Road and Trafalgar Square in the memory –
and the grim primness of Bloomsbury, Virginia Woolf's burgers –
I didn't even look – woosh down the tunnel to Seven Sisters –
back out at Church St NE16 – then down a pipe to Auckland
that Vincent Ward dug for a film – but reverse the time shift –
hundreds of years ago where outrigger ships moored
on the white sands of the Waitemata Harbour (the name means
glistening waters) where the land gave a huge volcanic sigh
bubbled into a miniature Fuji grew into the mountain
of red pohutukawa blossoms in every Aucklander's heart

17 *it's all been done before, eh*

yeah it's all been done before Trev
the great epics – odes to the explorers' gumboots and all –
I could tell you a tale or two but they've been said before
that's what he says eh – the professor who's read everything
he says everything's been done like a dinner
and you can't basically say anything new
except when you write about tiny little things
that no one else ever thought of writing about
because they didn't seem important then
so that's why they're important now: we're
mopping up the gravy and the gristle
off the real poets' plates – there's no point apparently
in writing odes and epics anymore –
although I do remember the good dry feeling of my feet
in warm socks in my gumboots in the rain
so bugger him

IV

For Fires

Song

FOR ANNE

An Irish song heard on National Public Radio:
I am stretched on your grave
and will lie there forever

The earth is filled with us.
So the ocean.
Voices filled with earth and water.

Trees move with the seasons.
Boats smart with time's slap.
So many voices move these.

Yet I cup my hands on the soil
and kiss it like your breasts.

Tell myself you'll wait there for me.

Boyle Abbey

(NEAR GALWAY)

Walls neatly bitten by time.

Stain and glass windows gone.

Stones supporting air.

Across the road is my bed and breakfast.

A priest has his morning meal.

I'd like to talk with him but
lack the words.

Heart Wounds

Why did we race the freeway at 3am and burn strapped to our seats
with the road worker friend and father whose face disintegrated as we struck him?

Why did we – to manipulate, interest, excite you?
Why get involved in this?

We're just the charred pieces of flesh left by the lightning of an event.

If I could I'd set up a MASH tent, dive under
to my personal monster, wring its stomach until it vomited back
my heart just so I could get you an answer.

And I'd be quick enough to stop us racing.

Take

AFTER MARINA TSVETAEVA

They took that mountain – the central pillar of the house
and quarried it away – took its granite entrails
to divine empire – and empire we read with a RP plum
whose stone bobbled in the male throats of the radio announcers –

took that lake and made it a marina for yachties
to sign the water, sign sign signing with a florid sailor's flutter
with the broadcasting corporation commentary to record it

took that forest and turned it in like a POW to Britain
with lopped limbs with the spine smoothed of knots
to be plonked in frigates for POWs to admire its girth

took the sermons on human rights and shoved it down our children
till they were daydream believers in an imperial matrix
where all light emanated from the monarch's sceptre
the Christmas Day microphone

took our throats with our land and their broadcasts
took almost everything except
the wisdom of our eyes

we see their racism everywhere
it lives on

Kowhaiwhai

I didn't understand the pattern before I started painting
even as my pencil etched the template on the wood
and the lines emerged in greyscale

I put down a white undercoat to seal the timber
so the curlicues, and curves, emerged from under.
I traced the red first – filled the ovals
and some of the edges with my children's brushes

the ones I'd bought at the hardware store
were too large – the loose bristles flung paint everywhere

It was my children's tips I needed – fine Crayola
that delighted in the paint drop – these red ones
that I smeared in the same direction because I was an artist!

Then onto the black – the major colour – three layers
black on black on black spilling out of the Polynesian nights
again with the Crayola bristles – some parts of the black

were triangles like outrigger sails – others smoothed
the passage between shapes like orifices – and the white
came out! I painted the white again

into living layers – dazzled my eyes as they emerged
from the red cave of the bloody nights – some kind of plant
these white lines some kind of fern

some kind of paddle too
or fingers grabbing the red and black

I could see genitalia here
Sperm and receptacles
Patterns bowing

And my applause for us

Love Poem

The night spent cloaked in rain and denim
reading Whitman and Sexton,
the scent of earth page on pages, gravemound flowers'
sweating to days' decay of unread passings, clumsy thumbings,
                        thick eyes at the anglepoise:
menstruation at forty marked in a heavy pencil
by a poor student, phallus and incest underlined as if
recounting a fairytale,
neglecting Anne for Sexton; Whitman on the rocks,
laureate, word-fisher, fine lines rolled
               like strong cigarettes,
spray tipped with sunset.
                  Orgasm in man and woman. The poem. Orgasm.
      Me an egotist tinkering with syllables and cricketing keys.
Find me a sonnet! Get me another word please.
         And there's nothing democratic about it!
         Nothing of the commercial magnificents,
boulevards and tall towers,
ships with long hauls of spice grape and singing nations,
men embracing women without contradiction embracing men,
woman instructing her desires,
         candles being lit and blown,
      smooth rub-cuddling of clean bodies
in large beds, breast cupped by hand,
            penis by fingers,
penetration of the saturated hips,
          and depth.
Held truly, she belongs to this great longing
              spelt in this.

close to you

Ovid's *The Art of Love* is filled with brute pressure
yet his advice has circulated for a couple of millennia
the stars he talks about are the ones that fill our planetariums
and our screens – Tom and Penelope for instance
who briefly replaced Nicole – if only he had some sulphur
to toss on their fire – I think Ovid
would have found him too good a husband
should have sprung Penelope from
her scallop shell before the parting
and sworn past the red tresses
of his beautiful goddess wife
that he'd never do it again

mother and child

she blinked to see the blood-red filtered
living room she floated in. no
mask and snorkel. no surface breaks.
only time and growth to mark her.

the forest that rose in her gave way to ocean
and surf edged shore. her mind grew more.
large enough her nose pushed out
into the light her mother knew.

she knew the circles of clockwork news:
white headed night, gold headed day
and all the spin between them:
voices filled with earth and water.

she knew the amazement of stars
birds clouds the wheels that turned them
up and over into bursts of laughter
thunder rain sparks and coping chants.

come out smooth like a barking seal
come out fast so your mum will heal
give your breath to our breath singing
above your mother's belly.

stepping stones

our children brought home some cement stepping stones
made at school – they used plastic ice cream tubs for moulds,

sand from the beach to lay the concrete on, and quick drying cement.
I know these things because I asked them. they inspired me to make a new path

for our backyard with their help. on the sand we laid pebbles,
colourful shells, speckled marbles, in no particular pattern,

using the base of a plastic flowerpot. then we mixed
gravel cement and water in a bucket and poured the slurry

over our patterns in the sand. after a day we turned
the first base over. it was round, with the patterns we dreamt

for our feet and eyes to fit. we repeated the feat
over several weekends until our path was longer.

the view from my office

clouds graze the hilltops like sheep
then a curtain of light parts them

v's escalate to the ridge the cloud nibbles
and then I see the hand, resting against the hillside

in the middle ground – fingers halfway out
of the bush-covered earth – it's enormous

below are houses and a university
in the foreground are tall buildings and stacks

Mānoa Campus, Honolulu 2004

purgatory

Tangaroa spread the seas
so we may cast and haul our nets inshore –
we fear the deeps, respect you for them
so no need to prove anything oh great father

Tāne Mahuta ruler of the birdsong and the branches
we ask you for shelter here in this cathedral
made for a very catholic communion
cast a cloak of feathers on us

Papatuanuku earth mother with child
give us an instant an instant
to turn this world on its spire-
tower-cottage-condo-metro'd head

the whole global culture flipped with the touch
of a discreet pedal and Aotearoa
of flightless birds, communist waka,
and a GDP one-fifth of the flipped other

come swinging back and locked to the top

Ahi Kā – The House of Ngā Puhi

We light the poem and breathe out
    the growing flames. Ahi kā. This
        is our home – our fire. Hot tongues out

– pukana – turn words to steam. This
    fish heart is a great lake on a
        skillet. Ahi kā! Ahi kā!

Keep the fire. The sun's rays are ropes
    held down by Māui's brothers.
        They handed down ray by burning

ray to each other every
    day – we keep the home fires burning
        every day. Mountains of our

house are its pillars – I believe
    in the forces that raised them here.
        Ahi kā burnt onto summits

char in the land, ahi kā dream,
    long bright cloud brilliant homeland.
        Ahi kā our life, ahi kā

carried by the tribe's forever-story
    firing every lullaby.
        Shadows shrink in our hands' quiver

as we speak – ahi kā sing fire
    scoop embers in the childhood sun
        stare into molten shapes and see

people – building, sailing, farming –
  see them in the flames of our land
      see them in this forever light

no tears only fire for ahi
  kā no weeping only hangi pits
      no regrets just forgiveness and

a place for the fire – it's our song
  to sing – ahi kā – got to keep
      singing the shadows away – ha!

the crackling page

my poetry is a fire –
if I close my mouth I will die

Poems from Another Century, for Parihaka

1 Graffiti

I am one last translation of the land
that has existed beyond all
genealogies beyond the earth.
The signature. Like the cloth
makes the man, so the land makes me.
Te Whiti and Tohu Kakahi
are of a long line, many acres,
connected to the land. The newcomers
have scribbled me over them,
over land, everywhere.

2 Akhmatova

Leningrad. The siege. An exit here
from skeleton city: a line tossed across
the Soviet Union by a poet who writes of Dante,
the immensity of love.

So very fine to bring back the siege,
to drop a curtain splattered in it,
a Soviet winter drawn in the muscles
of a little throat. A stray thought dressed

in the suffering of millions.
Obvious. Brutal. When the apothecary draws bullets
from flesh into her pan, she writes.
As I read her *1940* she writes.

3 John Bryce

Yes it's a beggar of a trip, but there's an election again.
Can't have the natives getting uppity
now that we've got the upper hand.
The bloody cheek of George to liken me
to Caesar! There's nothing like a few guns, and shells,
to show who's boss. Bloody George! That's the last time
I talk to him. Never again!
(I prefer the jibes by Jessie Mackay – RS.)

4 1995

As he told us I could feel it.
We saw the town of Parihaka
inside this marae.
As he told us I could feel it.
I could feel the artillery
pointed down on us –
knew if I put a foot wrong
they would shoot us all.

5 Te Whiti o Rongomai and Tohu Kakahi

I know only their reputations.
Monuments to them. People of Parihaka.
And signs of powerful peace.

6 Big Voice / Little Voice

i Big Voice

I'm big I'm six, so I am not afraid.
I have my skipping rope, and my hair is tied
                                   in braids.
My friend is here. He turns the rope
as we sing our song. I hope the horses
                                 on the road
won't hang around for long. Because!

ii Little Voice

We can feel them coming. The horses' feet,
and the guns on wheels, make the ground rumble.

We keep skipping and singing.
The soldiers get close enough to touch us.
But we keep skipping and singing.
The soldiers aren't very friendly.

They yell at us.
One picks me up and drops me on the roadside.
His friends laugh at me. Say I'm fat.
Then the rumbling starts again.
My friend gets stood on by a horse.
I feel very scared.

7 After the elections

Grey returns to Mansion House.
Bryce to the Capital.
Rousseau writes, 'Man is born free,
and everywhere he is in chains.'

8

There are ways of looking at a situation
so that heroes are drawn, and villains scratched
in lamp-black.
I think of the Hawaiian Queen Liliʻuokalani
imprisoned for her signature, and of the signatories
to our Treaty.
How they caused us to scratch.
And bow and scrape. Some
bent like horse-hair bows:
many snapped.
Yet in silence there is power.
In peace there is power.
In living we have power.
Being alive and human
(yes even that was questioned)
we remember Parihaka.
And we are reminded of our power.

9 The free world

I return to Leningrad.
Remember Akhmatova's poem
for the city, and for London.

I cannot explain the association.
It is so obscure and so obvious.

our country

had a beautiful birth shared by lovers
memory of its light carries us through today

and the propaganda of the *Herald* – the tablet
of a Grey imperium – it has a racist's eye for the unaware guy:
Don Brash tells: why I played the race card;
What's eating Pakeha; The verdict from the street – we've had enough;
Project runs the gauntlet of iwi consultation.

Still the birth was beautiful and the baby was beautiful too.
The long white cloud cloaked her little shoulders
like sheep wool. We still have the pictures of the baby
and remember her with pride: our greatest love
our country. New Zealand is still our child.

We made her with our mixed history and blood.
We will always be joined by her.

Notes

p.8, 'Tāne retrieves the baskets of knowledge'
Tāne – the Maori deity credited with bringing knowledge to humanity

p.10, 'Gods and Oysters'
Tangaroa – the Maori oceanic deity
waka – vessel
'face twisted . . . ee ya ha ha' – this facial contortion or pukana is typically performed in the haka, a war dance

p.26, 'The Great Hall'
The Great Hall is part of the old University of Canterbury complex in Christchurch, New Zealand. Marsden conducted the first church service in New Zealand in 1814.

p.28, 'Mai'
I am indebted to Dame Anne Salmond's chapter 'A Tahitian at the Opera' from her book The Trial of the Cannibal Dog.

p.36, 'Ocean Birth'
Moana Nui a Kiwa – the Pacific Ocean

p.49, 'Take'
take – the Maori word for 'cause'

p.50, 'Kowhaiwhai'
A kowhaiwhai pattern adorns the painted rafters of meeting houses, and contains many curvilinear motifs.

p.58, 'Ahi Kā – The House of Ngā Puhi'
Ahi kā – refers to a person's right to land, so long as they maintain their presence, or 'home fire'
pukana – a fierce facial contortion where the tongue is extended
'sun's rays are ropes' – the culture-hero Māui slowed the journey of the sun to provide lengthier days, with the help of his brothers
'mountains of our house' – refers to the House of Ngā Puhi, the Northland tribe
'long bright cloud' – refers to the Maori name for New Zealand, land of the long white cloud, Aotearoa
'hands' quiver' – refers to the quivering motions of the hands in action songs
hangi – an earth oven